THE TAN PANTSUIT PURSUIT

FOILED BY THE FINAL VOTE

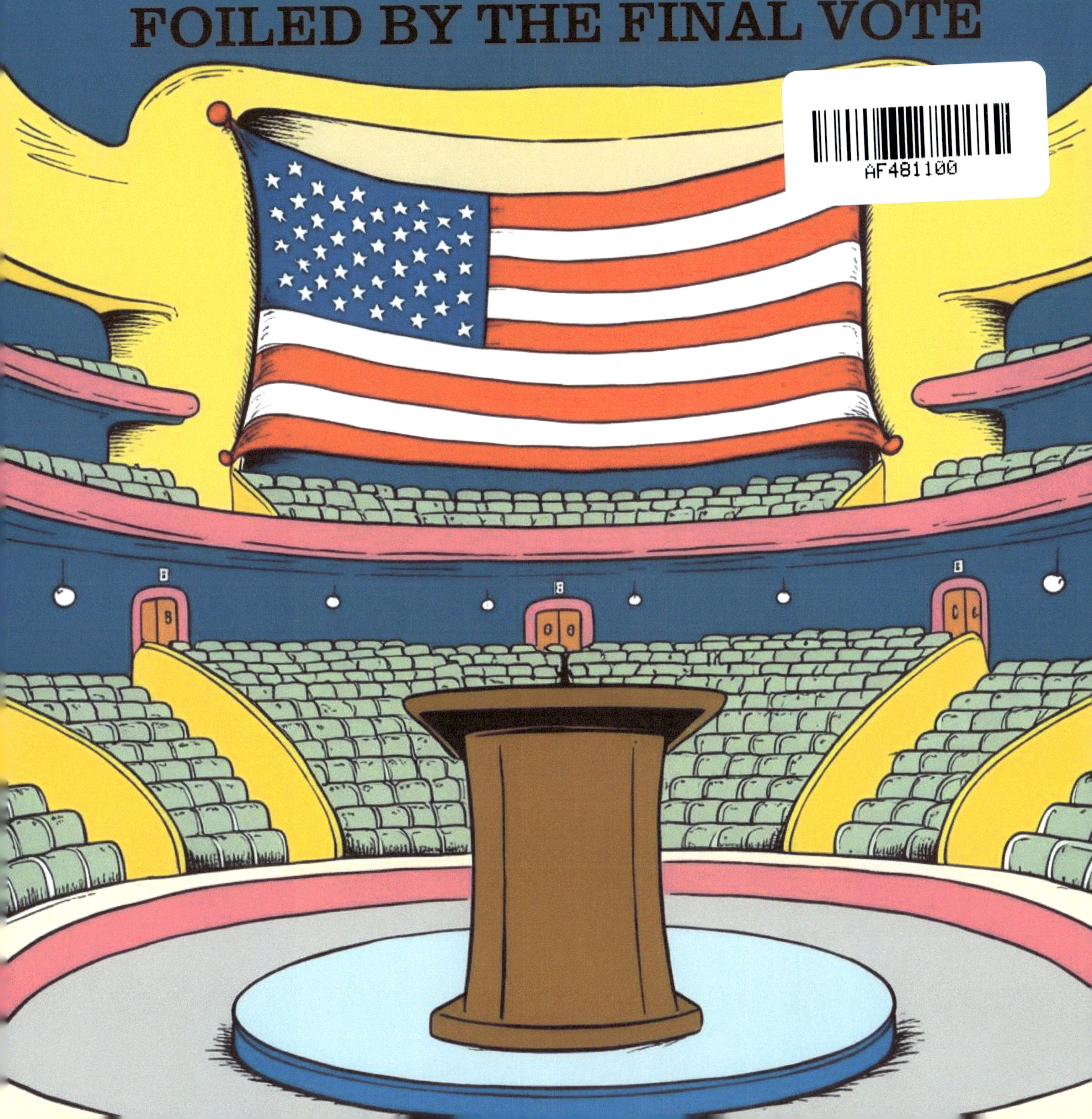

Dedicated to those who drank from the hose as kids and now casually sip the tears of America's most fragile snowflakes.

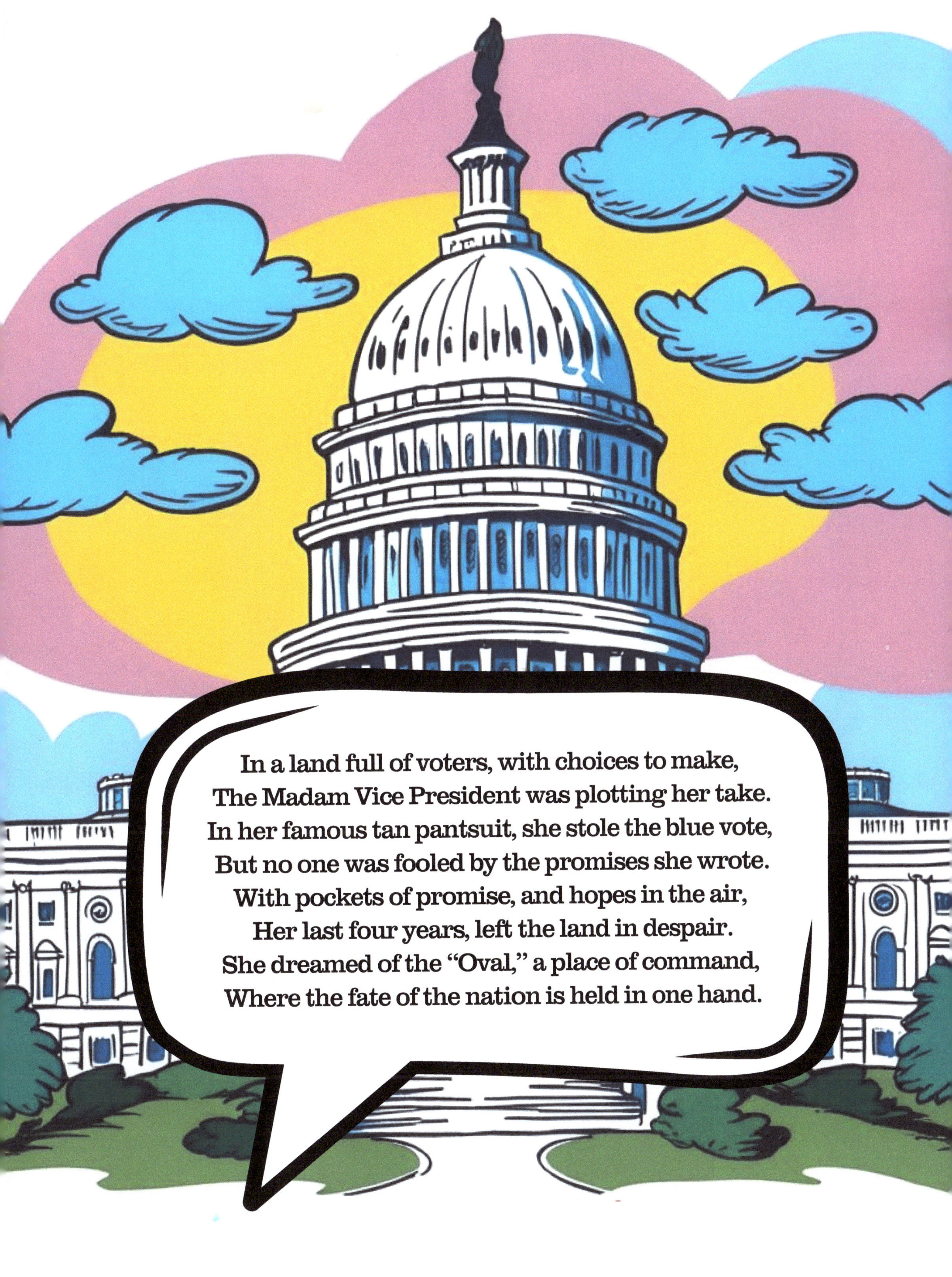

In a land full of voters, with choices to make,
The Madam Vice President was plotting her take.
In her famous tan pantsuit, she stole the blue vote,
But no one was fooled by the promises she wrote.
With pockets of promise, and hopes in the air,
Her last four years, left the land in despair.
She dreamed of the "Oval," a place of command,
Where the fate of the nation is held in one hand.

Her name on the ballot, no efforts to make,
A last-minute heist, no votes to partake.
Now many will argue the country's misled,
That she's done all she could do, to stay firmly aHEAD.
She hit the road on the campaign trail,
Hoping her victory would surely prevail.
With her team in control, they scripted and wrote,
They fed her some lines, like a fish on a boat.

They prepped her and posed her to jump in the race,
And stealing the vote was a disgrace to embrace.
"Just smile and look charming, and wave with a cheer!
And practice your answers; the cameras are near!"
Dressed up for a job she was not meant to take,
The pant suit can't hide that her speeches were fake.

Her speeches were tricky, like tangled-up thread,
With words that spun circles, leaving logic for dead.
She speaks in word salad and rehearsed all her lines;
Her words twist and turn, but no meaning aligns.

"I'm here for the people, I'll make changes, no doubt,
And the last four years weren't as bad as they shout."

"Trust me!" she shouted, "I know what to do!
Remember y'all, I'm from the middle class too!"

The debate was a circus, with an end in defeat,
She stumbled on questions like a drunk on his feet.
Her answers were slippery, like a breakdancer's glide,
She'd spin and she'd flip, keeping truths pushed aside.

On her journey, to visit the many swing states,
She avoided the press and sealed her own fate.
She'd only give answers when two could confide,
With her running mate always close by her side.
The crowds and the people grew tired of her game,
her answers got harder for her to explain.
With questions like arrows, they flew from the crowd,
Yet her answers still shady, her voice far from loud.

When asked about budgets, she'd stammer and sway,
Like a mime with no script, she had nothing to say.
Her mind was a tangle, her thoughts in a race,
Like a mouse on a wheel, just stuck in one place.
The crowds began buzzing, their doubts taking hold,
Her strategy felt like a short story half-told.
She'd promise the moon, and she'd promise the stars,
But her words were all tangled, like mangled up cars.

"I've got a solution, just trust me once more,
I'll make all the changes I didn't before."
"Let's find someone better!" they shouted with dread,
"Her plans aren't so grand; they're all full of lead."
She'd twist and she'd turn, she'd dodge and she'd weave,
And the voters just watched, with no hope to believe.

PANTSUIT
FOR
PRESIDENT

She swiped the nomination without any work,
Her endorsements all came from supporters who twerk.
Her last four years left Americans broke,
And her message to them was, "We must be more woke!"
Young voters are stupid, she thinks so she said
She thought she was clever, and now they vote red.
She tried to explain her logic you see,
"Do you really think you fell out of a coconut tree?"

In a tan pantsuit so bold, she strutted with flair,
With pockets of promise and hopes in the air.
"Oh look at me!" with a twirl and a spin,
"This suit shows my power, my confidence within!"
But the crowd saw right through it, they saw the disguise,
A suit can not mask her history of lies.
And while it was stylish, it lacked any spark,
Just like her campaign, it fell short of the mark.
So there she stood, in her pantsuit, so neat,
But the charm wore off fast, and it couldn't compete.

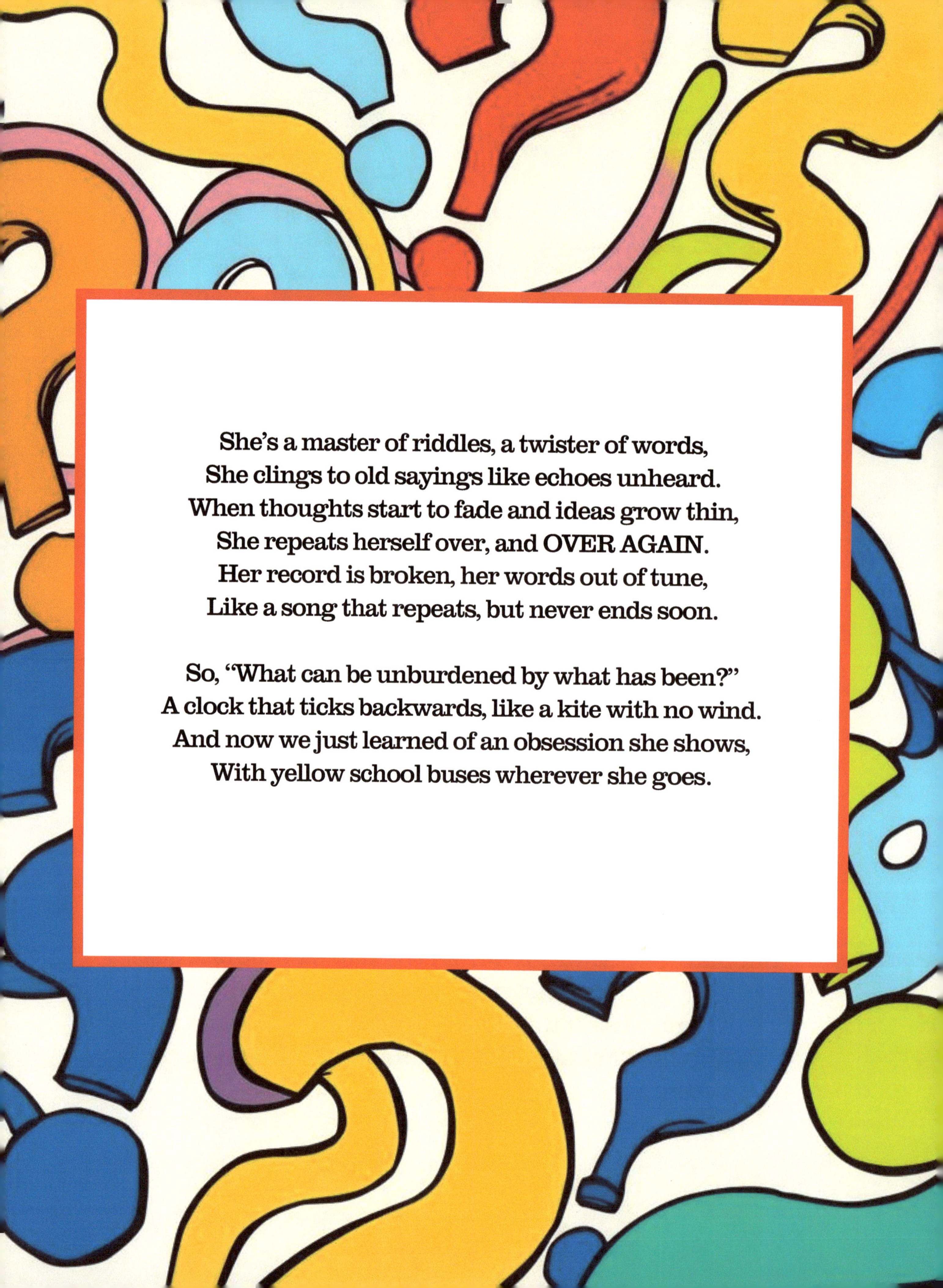

She's a master of riddles, a twister of words,
She clings to old sayings like echoes unheard.
When thoughts start to fade and ideas grow thin,
She repeats herself over, and OVER AGAIN.
Her record is broken, her words out of tune,
Like a song that repeats, but never ends soon.

So, "What can be unburdened by what has been?"
A clock that ticks backwards, like a kite with no wind.
And now we just learned of an obsession she shows,
With yellow school buses wherever she goes.

SCHOOL BUS
SCHOOL

She threw A-list rallies to sway the crowd's vote,
With hopes of big concerts to keep her afloat.
She worked all the angles, pulling in all the fame,
Hoping all of the cameos would fuel her campaign.
No matter the venue, the speaker or scene,
The nation distrusted the left side regime.
"Immigration is bad!" they yelled and they screamed,
Leaving voters to question the American Dream.
The people were restless, with issues galore,
The crime and the debt made folks worry much more.

On Election Day, she stayed out of sight,
No banners or stars, no dancing that night.
The party went on, her supporters did cheer,
But she stayed back at home, like a ghost, disappeared.
The votes came in fast, and the numbers were clear —
Her time had passed on, it was no longer near.
The people had spoken, they made their demand,
Her tan suit was hollow, just like her command.
No more did they need her tangled word chase,
Nor the giggle she gave, or that grin on her face.

So, she packed up her suit, knowing this was the end,
A time to move on and stop playing pretend.
"Goodbye, tan suit, with your pockets of woe,
You were unable to save me when the red wave did flow."
With a sigh and a glance, she set it aside,
A reminder that fashion can not turn the tide.

The votes were all counted, the math was all done,
She realized the people had chosen someone.
And a big red wave came, as a strong rising tide,
And all of a sudden there was no place to hide.

Her shortcut to power was clear as could be,
But the people saw through it, and didn't agree.
She tried to outwit them with a bait and switch scheme,
But they didn't buy in to the left side regime.
So here's the big lesson that all should now know:
You can't fool the people with a suit or a show.

For no matter the tactics, the tricks, or the lies,
The truth will come out, and the people will rise.
And when the dust settles, and the ballots are cast,
The line in the sand will stand strong, and steadfast.
You can talk in circles, with your laugh so bizarre,
But in the end, it's the people who decide who's in charge.

So now we look forward to a familiar command,
With hopes and dreams of a safe, prosperous land.
Back in the Oval, he is set to begin,
With a team and plan to **Make America Great Again!**

Punchline Press Co
Publication Year: 2024
ISBN: 979-8-218-99012-1
Edition: First Edition